# Forgotten Civilizations
## *Decoding Untold Stories*

# Table of Contents

# Chapter 1. Introduction

Embark on a remarkable journey through the echoes of time with our special report on "Forgotten Civilizations: Decoding Untold Stories". This richly detailed narrative will guide you through the unexplored tales and enigmatic remnants of civilizations long vanished. Unearth their ingenious innovations, complex societal structures, and captivating cultures that have commanded the sands of time. This is not just a report, it's an adventure that weaves together archaeological findings, historical documentation, and cutting-edge research for an enthralling exploration of humanity's unremembered past. Can you hear the whispers of the forgotten? Discover their stories and the legacy they've left for us to uncover — a history that demands to be brought to light. This special report is a treasure trove for the curious mind—your passport to the past is just a click away!

# Chapter 2. Unearthing the Invisible: Introduction to Forgotten Civilizations

In an all but silent world, untouched landscapes sprawl wide and immense—sweeping plains, craggy mountain ranges, scorched deserts, and teeming jungles. These are not your usual tourist destinations. These are the mysterious corners of our planet where countless civilizational footprints lie buried beneath layers of earth, striving to narrate their tale.

## 2.1. Echoes in the Sands

Hundreds of thousands of years have carved their history upon our world, with civilizational pasts flickering like starlight across the epochs. Buried deep within the sands, curried in the heart of the mountains, or lost in the dense wilderness—they whisper to us tantalizing tales of cultures magnificent, societies complex, and lives lived in shades we can now barely comprehend. Preserved beneath the surface lie architectural masterpieces, ingenious tools, expressive artworks, and thought-provoking written treatises—each a silent testament to the inexorable march of human progress.

## 2.2. The Lost Chronicles

An awakening understanding of dated technologies, societal systems, or artistic expressions often illuminates the overlooked aspects of our ancestors' lives. Too frequently, our own cultural and historical biases cloud perceptions of these erstwhile societies. In truth, these forgotten societies were rich in knowledge and innovation, complex in societal structures, and frequently more sophisticated than acknowledged. They navigated life's adversities with the tools, knowledge, and wisdom of their time, leaving behind fragments of narratives waiting to be pieced together and appreciated.

## 2.3. The Archaeological Quest

Archaeology, our tool for engaging with these echoes of the past, is painstaking work. Methodical, intensely detailed, requiring equal parts of physical tenacity and intellectual dexterity, it reveals findings not just of stone and bone, but also of the dreams, aspirations, and daily lives of beings long departed. Through the use of technology, anthropologists and archaeologists give voice to these relics. Sophisticated imaging systems, advanced dating methods, and analytic tools are enabling us to penetrate the haze of time, offering us unprecedented insight into the forgotten chapters of humanity.

## 2.4. Deciphering the Past

History is never as linear as it might seem, and its interpretations are manifold. Our forgotten civilizations present a diverse and complex narrative, laden with hidden subtleties. Understanding these tales necessitates a multidisciplinary approach, drawing upon linguistic analysis, climate studies, genetic research, and cherished oral traditions circulating across generations. It is only through this eclectic amalgamation of paths and perspectives can we hope to form a comprehensive picture of our species' untold journey.

## 2.5. Narrating the Untold

The stories the forgotten civilizations have to tell are not merely of their times, but ours as well. As we unveil their mysteries, we question our historigraphical assumptions, reevaluate our collective identity, and expand our understanding of what it means to be human. Their chronicles engender a sense of shared heritage, revealing the interconnected narratives of our species in ways we could not have imagined. In their successes and struggles, we find echoes of our own, paving the path to introspect, learn, and improve.

## 2.6. Skeletons and Stones

Material evidence serves as the bedrock to our understanding of forgotten civilizations. Excavation sites, almost like crime scenes, offer invaluable clues into the past. Remains of settlements, palaces, streets, and markets outline establishments of power and societal interactions. Expressive wall murals, intricate jewelry, symbols inscribed on stone or ceramic—all testimony to their artistic and intellectual prowess. Every bone unearthed, every tool discovered, every symbol decoded, offers a tiny but precious piece of an enormous jigsaw puzzle that, once solved, gradually unveils the grand panorama of lost civilizations.

## 2.7. Influences and Impressions

Traces of these forgotten societies persist in modern culture, woven subtly into the fabric of contemporary societies. From belief systems to language patterns, architectural styles to scientific principles, their wisdom underpins aspects of human life today in ways unrecognized. The symbols and stories from the yesteryears continue to shape identities, influence arts, and inspire innovations. Recognizing these traces and influences provides a unique lens to observe our history, demonstrating the enduring power of these civilizations that refuse to be entirely forgotten.

## 2.8. Setting the Stage

In this exploration of forgotten civilizations, we must set the stage to immerse ourselves completely in their contexts. We need an appreciation for their epochs—the ambit of their geography, the challenges of their climates, the circumstances of their eras—all major contributors to their cultural and sociological evolution. By understanding the impact of these elements on the civilizations, we stabilize the foundation upon which the specifics of their lives can be explored, creating a realistic picture of their lived experiences.

As we delve deeper into the uncharted territories of the long gone, let us commit to peeling back the layers with an open mind and a boundless curiosity. The journey might be arduous, and the mountains to scale high. But in rising to these challenges, we may just be rewarded with a treasure trove of collective wisdom and a human story that is as complex, diverse, and fascinating as it is ours. The civilizations remembered forgot not because they ceased to exist, but because we failed to remember. It's time we retrieved their narrations and recognized their contributions to the grand narrative of humanity. The tales of civilizations past are out there, whispering in the winds, breathing in the artifacts, written in the sands—waiting for you to discover.

# Chapter 3. Once Thriving, Now Silent: The Enigma of the Indus Valley

In the expansive, arid expanse of what is now Pakistan and Northwestern India, a civilization sprouted around the bronze age, one of the earliest citadels of urbanization and sophisticated state governance we know to date. The story of the Indus Valley civilization is one of remarkable prosperity, intricacy, and unexplained disappearance, leaving behind a legacy engraved in thousands of archaeological artifacts, just waiting to speak.

## 3.1. Inception and Evolution

The Indus Valley civilization, thought to have begun around 3300 B.C.E., had a lifespan that lasted until about 1300 B.C.E., enclosing the bronze age within its temporality. A civilization that mustered thoughtfully planned cities, a system of standardized weights and measures, intricate drainage and sanitation systems, and a still undeciphered script, the Indus Valley civilization was a testament to human innovation at its dawn.

Unearthed bricks, uniform in size, tell tales of meticulous city planning and construction. Harappa and Mohenjo-daro, the civilization's two largest cities, a remarkable testimony to this civilization's technological advancement and complex societal structure. Streets laid out in a precise grid pattern, fortified citadels, even a system of homogenous brick sizes: this was a civilization led by order, uniformity, and possibly, collective democratic decision-making processes.

Further, archaeologists have gathered extensive evidence of advanced municipal planning. The Indus Valley civilization boasted a comprehensive sewage and drainage system, accentuating advanced knowledge of urban hygiene and sanitation. Moreover, noticed within the ruins are large public wells and evidence of what seems to be an early form of city-wide water distribution.

## 3.2. The Unsolved Script

Among the sealed mysteries of the Indus Valley civilization is their script. Despite the abundance of seals, pottery shards, and copper tablets inscribed with this script, a cohesive understanding of its content remains elusive.

The civilization's writing system, etched onto seals or copper tablets, doesn't associate with any other known ancient script. Though attempts at decipherment have hypothesized that it may be an early Dravidian language, verification and further study are needed to confirm this theory.

## 3.3. Twists of Trade and Economy

What suggests an expansive trade network are the wide variety of material artifacts discovered. This includes a collection of precious gems such as lapis lazuli, turquoise, and carnelian, alongside silvers, shells, and ceramics. Additionally, standardized systems of weights and measures contribute to the hypothesis that the Indus Valley civilization was a thriving hub of trade.

Evidence such as seals, beads, pottery, and bronze implements strewn across Ancient Mesopotamian archaeological sites, indicate the signs of a long-distance trade relationship. The Mesopotamian records reference trade with "Meluhha," an unknown region that many scholars are tempted to identify with the Indus Valley based on the geographical and chronological corroborations.

## 3.4. Enigmatic Religiosity and Beliefs

Hints of religious practices provide further insight into the civilization. Unearthed figurines and seals depict animals, humans and oddly, humanoid figures mingling with beasts, suggesting animistic practices. The infamous "Pashupati Seal," bearing the figure of a possibly seated deity flanked by animals, has led to conjectures about ties with early forms of Hinduism.

It is, however, essential to exercise caution while studying religion through the archaeological lens because of the implicit subjectivity and cultural frames imposed on such interpretations. The civilization's perceptions of the divine, their belief systems, and their spiritual practices are yet to be thoroughly decoded.

## 3.5. The Disintegration Enigma

What shrouds the Indus Valley civilization in further intrigue is its sudden apparent disappearance around 1700 BCE. A decline in material culture, a decreased complexity in societal structures, and subsequently, evidence of abandonment reflects this decline. However, the cause behind such a downfall is a mystery yet unwoven by historians and archaeologists.

Multiple theories attempt to explain this, ranging from invasions to environmental disasters such as floods, shifts in the river's course, or frequent droughts. Some also hypothesize a gradual societal collapse, whereby the civilization could have gradually degraded due to internal crises such as political instability or economic collapse.

However, none of these theories are conclusive, and the tales of the end of this civilization remain embedded within the unspoken narratives of archaeological remains and environmental footprints. Therefore, the downfall of the Indus Valley civilization remains a puzzle for time to unravel.

# 3.6. Lasting Legacy

Tales of the Indus Valley forms the prehistoric episode of South Asia's extensive historical saga, a canvas that modern day India, Pakistan, and Bangladesh sprung from. This civilization left a legacy of architectural, societal, and naturally induced changes on this landscape. Communities probably lingering within echoes of this long-gone civilization might allow us to thread together the sprawling tapestry of South Asian history, from its dawn to its multicultural present.

The Indus Valley civilization, once thriving, now silent, continues to occupy the corridors of unnamed history. Yet, it resonates in the collective consciousness of humanity as one of the emblems of our early civilizational prowess. Still, they whisper to us, their descendants millennia apart, through the echoes of artifacts, structures, and an unclaimed script—a saga awaiting further exploration, a civilization inviting us into its silenced narrative.

# Chapter 4. The Mesoamerican Marvels: Olmec, Zapotec and More

Enigmatic and deeply intriguing, the Mesoamerican civilization, encapsulating the Olmec, Zapotec, and beyond, woos the imagination with its distinctive art, advanced science, and profound civilization values, which have left imprints on the sands of time. With the following explorative journey, delve deep into the inscrutable past of this fascinating region and its people.

## 4.1. The Dawn Breakers: The Olmec

The Olmec civilization, frequently hailed as Mesoamerica's 'Mother Culture', thrived from approximately 1400 to 400 BCE. Primarily occupying a region along Mexico's Gulf coast, the Olmec civilization's remnant colossal stone heads remain as a testament to their artistic mastery and a silent attestation to their intriguing past.

The economy was primarily agriculture-driven, with the Olmecs cultivating a variety.

| Crop | Importance |
| --- | --- |
| Maize | Primary food source and sacred plant |
| Beans and Squash | Secondary staple crops |
| Cotton | Used in textile production |

Advanced irrigation and flood control systems were developed for efficient agriculture.

Embracing a theocratic rule, their social and religious lives were intricately intertwined. The reigns were supposedly in hands of ruler-priests who were seen as intermediaries between the spiritual and earthly realms.

The Olmec civilization is best known for its colossal stone heads, believed to be portraits of revered rulers. Sculpted from basalt, these heads are considered an engineering feat and a marvel of Olmec artistry.

# 4.2. The Cloud People: The Zapotec

The Zapotec civilization, known as the 'Cloud People', marked their presence in the Oaxaca Valley around 500 BCE. Monte Alban, their capital city, is an architectural wonder, perched atop a series of artificial terraces.

With their elaborate hieroglyphic writing and a comprehensive calendar system, the Zapotec left behind artefacts rich in informational value. Notably, they developed the 'Danza de las Voladoras' — the Dance of the Flyers, believed to serve as a communication with the gods.

Agriculture was the heart of the Zapotec society, with the communal work in the farms playing a significant role.

| Crop | Importance |
|---|---|
| Maize | Primary food source and ceremonial crop |
| Beans and Squash | Secondary staple crops |
| Agave | Used in textile production and beverages |

Introducing terracing and irrigation, they maximized their arable land. The Zapotec government structure was a complex blend of city-states, each headed by a distinct ruling elite. The power was shared among councils and primary families.

Zapotec art and architecture reflect their spiritual beliefs, with building designs often aligning with celestial bodies. Their tombs, adorned with intricate frescoes, offer deep insight into their funeral rites and beliefs about death and the afterlife.

# 4.3. Reflections of the Past

Our journey through the Olmec and Zapotec civilizations enlightens us about the sophistication inherent in early societies. Unraveling the tapestry of their cultures allows us to appreciate their ingenuity, resourcefulness, and the profound connection they harbored with the environment.

These civilizations' significant advancements in agriculture, writing systems, and art bear witness to their legacy contributing to the larger Mesoamerican narrative. Their ruins stand as silent yet persistent reminders of their existence, echoing stories of a time lost in oblivion.

The Olmec and Zapotec civilizations are an integral part of humanity's grand narrative, offering compelling testament to the indefatigability of the human spirit. They showcase how our ancestors triumphed over their environment, innovated, and created robust societal structures — a call for us to learn and remember.

Such exploration of forgotten civilizations invites, above all, a respect, a reverence for past cultures, and a realization of their intricate threads woven into the fabric of our modern world. As we unlock these civilizations' secrets, we decipher more about our shared human story — illuminating the path that has led us to the world we know today.

# Chapter 5. Glories of Çatalhöyük: Understanding An Ancient Metropolis

An aura of mystique surrounds the muddy mounds of Çatalhöyük, a Neolithic site located in the central plains of Turkey. First discovered by British archaeologist James Mellaart in the 1950s, these mounds conceal the striking remnants of one of the world's oldest known cities.

## 5.1. The Discovery

The initial discovery of Çatalhöyük was a breakthrough, shedding light on the capabilities of ancient societies. When James Mellaart excavated the site between 1961 and 1965, he found robust evidence of a thriving civilization that resided in the region more than 9,000 years ago. Remarkably well-preserved artifacts and buildings painted a vivid picture of society, rebuking prior notions that complex social structures emerged only with the advent of agriculture.

## 5.2. Fascinating Facts: Vital Statistics

Çatalhöyük lasted for over a millennium, reaching its peak around 7000 BCE. It covered an area of 32 acres, with a population estimated between 5,000 and 7,000, making it a metropolis in terms of Neolithic settlements. It was a society built without the presence of conventional streets, a central public square, or significant fortifications.

## 5.3. A Close-Knit Community

This was a very close-knit community, where people inhabited houses clustered closely together. No separating spaces between the houses were left, and the residents instead navigated their city through roofs, entering their houses from above using ladders. Inside these structures, archaeologists discovered intricately decorated rooms with vibrant murals, reflecting a rich cultural and spiritual life.

## 5.4. Technological Innovations: Pottery and Obsidian

The people of Çatalhöyük made technological advancements in pottery and obsidian tools. The use of obsidian, a black volcanic glass, was widespread in the manufacture of sharp objects like arrowheads and cutting tools. Interestingly, Çatalhöyük was not just an end-user, but a major trade hub for obsidian.

## 5.5. Spiritual Beliefs and Practices

Symbols, particularly those featuring bulls, are evident throughout the site, etched into the walls or represented in statues. Many archaeologists believe these may have been central to the spiritual beliefs and practices of the society. The practice of burying their dead beneath the house floors has led to the conclusion that ancestor worship might have been preponderant.

## 5.6. The Decline of Çatalhöyük

The city began to decline around 6000 BCE. Several theories have been proposed for this change, with climate change and environmental degradation being primary suspects. But despite its fall, the legacy of Çatalhöyük lived on through its innovative designs, artistic expressions, and advanced technology.

## 5.7. Legacy and Impact

The echoed stories of Çatalhöyük provide invaluable insight into early urban living and the evolution of human societies. By unearthing understanding of how our ancestors lived, we shed light on the contextual background to today's city cultures and develop a deeper understanding of our roots.

## 5.8. Ongoing Excavation

Recent archaeological missions have sought to unravel more about Çatalhöyük's life and times. Guided by meticulous soil analyses, revolutionary remote sensing, and innovative techniques like micro-excavation, the archaeologists have been able to reconstruct a compelling narrative about this ancient civilization.

The whispers of Çatalhöyük tell stories of human resilience, creativity, and adaptivity in the face of changing climates, societal requirements, and demographic pressures. These narratives, etched into the folds of time, continually beckon us to explore, learn, and grow. But above all, they remind us of our shared humanity and the intricate tapestry of our collective past.

# Chapter 6. Grandeur of the Goths: Europe's Unseen Nomads

Often relegated to the shadows in popular historical narratives, the Goths were far more than Europe's unseen nomads. They were bearers and builders of a grandiosity, the likes of which span over centuries, leaving valuable insights into an ever-evolving civilization.

## 6.1. From Scandinavia to Gothic Kingdoms

Drawn from sources like Jordanes, a 6th-century Roman bureaucrat and historian, there's belief that the Goths originated from Scandinavia. Ancestral stories recount their journey from the glacial landscapes of the North to the bustling territories of Eastern Europe, as they sought fertile lands and better livelihoods.

On their meandering path, they absorbed elements from the numerous peoples they encountered, enriching their own cultural tapestry. This migration led to the creation of Gothic kingdoms, namely the Ostrogothic Kingdom in Italy and the Visigothic Kingdom in Iberian Peninsula, signs of a burgeoning civilization that dared to carve its own destiny in the face of a crumbling Roman Empire.

## 6.2. Society, Politics, and Economy

The Gothic society had its roots in tribal traditions, with each tribe led by a chieftain. However, as they interacted with the Romans, their societal structure evolved, imbibing elements of Roman administration and military organization, yet grounding them in their unique cultural context.

Agriculture, animal husbandry, crafting, and trade were economic mainstays. Open-air markets bustled with the trading of wares from the far reaches of the known world, signifying an extensive network of commerce.

# 6.3. Innovation at the Intersections of Culture

Perhaps the most striking aspect of the Goths was their ability to adapt and innovate. Existing at the crossroads of numerous civilizations, they did not resist change but embraced it, integrating aspects of Roman architecture, Persian artistry, and Celt wisdom.

The creation of the Wulfila bible, a translation of the Christian Bible into the Gothic language, was a momentous feat. It not only reveals about the Gothic literacy but also their technological prowess. The Codex Argenteus, a surviving silver-inked manuscript of this bible, reflect the sophistication and value of the language to their culture.

The architecture of the Goths also merits special attention. Although no "Gothic" buildings from the Gothic period have survived, their architectural influence is visible in the religious monumental buildings of the Romanesque and the medieval period, giving birth to the distinguished "Gothic Architecture".

# 6.4. Religion: Arianism versus Nicene Christianity

Religion played a significant role in the dynamics of the Gothic civilization. The Goths were initially Pagan, worshiping entities of nature. However, their interaction with the Romans led to their conversion to Arian Christianity, a form of Christianity considered heretical by the Roman Church.

This religious divergence resulted in a politically fraught relationship with Rome, who adhered to Nicene Christianity. Yet, it showcases the Gothic resilience in maintaining their chosen beliefs despite being in a socio-political minority.

# 6.5. The Fall of the Gothic Kingdoms

The eventual fall of the Gothic kingdoms is as interwoven with their interactions with external civilizations as their rise. Invasions, political instability, economic downturn, and religious strife contributed to the decline. However, they left behind a legacy that permeated the societal structures, languages, and cultures of Europe.

When we consider the Goths, they serve as a mirror reflecting the expansive horizon of human ability to adapt, innovate, and endure. Their story is a testament to civilization's ability to defy reductionist narratives and stereotyping.

It is with these narratives that the echoes of the Goths live on, whispering of a past where they weren't just the unseen nomads, but a civilization of congregation and conversion, of resilience and revolution. Through the grandeur of the Goths, we rediscover an untold chapter of Europe's history.

# Chapter 7. Beneath Sands and Seas: Lost cities of Atlit Yam and Thonis-Heracleion

Hidden from the world, submerged under the stretch of our boundless seas and masked beneath the shifting granules, are the legacies of civilizations past. Atlit Yam and Thonis-Heracleion, two pearls of forgotten history, concealed for a millennium beneath sands and seas, offer unique windows into the life and times that were.

## 7.1. Sea's Embrace: Atlit Yam

Atlit Yam, an archaeological marvel located off the coast of modern Israel, emerged from the sea's embrace in 1984. It had slumbered under the Mediterranean for about 9,000 years, languishing in oblivion until marine archaeologist Ehud Galili accidentally chanced upon it.

Artifacts from the settlement, including well-preserved houses, a ritual site, stone-paved areas, and more than 100 human skeletons, reflect the complexities of life during the late epipaleolithic period. Dated from around 6900 to 6300 BC, the settlement of Atlit Yam spans an impressive area of 40,000 square meters, submerged beneath up to 12 meters of sea water.

Mechanisms such as wild cereal exploitation, animal domestication, and cultivation of legumes reflected an evolutionary transition towards agriculture offering fresh insights into Neolithic Revolution – the momentous shift from hunter-gatherers to farm societies.

The location of Atlit Yam also suggests a close relationship between its inhabitants and the marine environment, hinted by a rectangular stone installation thought to be a water well, and a semi-circle of seven megaliths interpreted as a possible calendrical apparatus or ceremonial site. It was perhaps here, amid stone monuments and azure waves, that civilization explored its earliest spiritual and astronomical quests.

Another fascinating revelation from Atlit Yam involves a more macabre aspect – the grim portrait of health or, more precisely, disease. The skeletal remains, including the earliest known case of tuberculosis in history, underline disease burden, highlighting how the shift to sedentary life aggravated health challenges.

# 7.2. Sunken Splendor: Thonis-Heracleion

Cloaked in ancient papyrus tales and Classical historians' scrolls, Thonis-Heracleion was considered a myth until its rediscovery in 2000 by French archaeologist Franck Goddio. The city, a prominent trade and religious center of the Mediterranean world during the late period, was nestled at the mouth of the Canopic branch of the Nile, in present-day Aboukir Bay.

Thonis-Heracleion thrived from around the 8th century BC, peaking in the 4th and 3rd centuries BC. It played a dual role– as Heracleion, a prominent Greek port, and Thonis, a bustling Egyptian city – catering to the diverse cultural flux from the Mediterranean basin.

Resurrected from its watery grave, numerous magnificently preserved statues, steles, sarcophagi, and ritual offerings have surfaced. A stunning 5.4 meter statue of the god Happy, over 700 ancient anchors, gold coins, and more—all add to the fascinating historical puzzle of Thonis-Heracleion.

Thonis-Heracleion was a city of monumental religious significance. The grand temple of Amun, linked with Thonis-Heracleion through inscriptions, was central to ceremonies involving newly crowned pharaohs, the annual 'Mysteries of Osiris' event, and tax collection center for Egyptian and Greek Mediterranean trade — hence its nickname: 'the Egyptian Venice'.

The treasures of Thonis-Heracleion also speak of its fall. Likely due to the land's unstable clay and silt foundation, the city probably sank abruptly around the 2nd century AD. The catastrophic event, coupled with rising sea levels and seismic activities, consigned it to the abyss, only to be revealed centuries later.

Transcending the sands and seas, Atlit Yam and Thonis-Heracleion have proven archaeology's potent power to resurrect history. Through their silent stones and age-old artifacts, they invite us to witness the unchronicled nuances of human existence, challenging our understanding of societal evolution, cultural hybridity, and ecological frailty. As such, these lost cities continue their eternal dialogues about human progress and nature's might, leaving an imprint on our collective memory, inciting us to delve deeper into the entrancing realm of forgotten civilizations.

# Chapter 8. Trading Tracks: Unravelling the Nok Civilization

Deep in the heart of what is now known as Nigeria, an ancient civilization flourished long before the pyramids of Egypt were built. This ancient civilization, infamous yet hardly recognized beyond the scholarly world, is the Nok culture. Despite limited archeological evidence, the legacy of the Nok people survives in their enigmatic terra-cotta sculptures, and intriguing hints of formidable trading networks—the focus of this chapter.

## 8.1. The Terra-cotta Clues

The first knowledge of the Nok civilization came from the accidental discovery of terra-cotta figurines by tin miners in the Nok region of Nigeria in 1928. The miners stumbled upon pottery heads, which were discarded as irrelevant trinkets in the quest for tin. Later identified as the remnants of a forgotten civilization, these anthropomorphic sculptures depict individuals with elaborate hairstyles and jewelry, suggesting a complex societal structure and advanced craftsmanship. However, the Nok terra-cotta are much more than aesthetic masterpieces; they provide glimpses into the economic activities of this forgotten civilization, including crucial trading tracks.

## 8.2. Enigmatic Evidence of Trade

The evidence of trade in Nok culture emerges from the very existence of the terra-cotta figures. The sophisticated modeling techniques used to create these figures shows practical understanding of kiln firing that requires a substantial supply of wood. Given the location of Nok civilization in areas now classified as primarily Sahelian grasslands, experts agree that the extensive use of wood suggests a trade network capable of supplying such resources.

The Nok civilization was also involved in iron smelting, nearly 2,500 years before other African civilizations. The advanced weaponry and tools made from smelted iron imply possible trade relations with civilizations that held the ability to mine iron ores.

A closer look at the Nok artifacts reveals a more complex trading network. Some of the materials used, like mica, feldspar, and kaolinite, are not native to the Jos Plateau, where Nok was located, indicating that the Nok people traded with distant civilizations where these materials were abundant.

## 8.3. The Trading Channels

The Nok civilization, located on the Jos Plateau—a geographic crossroads—, exhibits connections with trading routes spanning various directions. Trade routes possibly extended west to the Niger River, east to the Benue River, and south to the Atlantic coast, thus opening the Nok civilization to a plethora of foreign influences and resources.

To the south, the Niger Delta was home to settlements known for their exquisite ivory and wood crafts, a possible trading partner for the detail-orriented Nok craftsmen. To the east, the Chad Basin, replete with abundant fish, grains, and livestock, could have been another productive trading connection, potentially enriching the Nok diet.

## 8.4. The External Trade Influences

Possessing little written records of the Nok civilization, scholars rely on artefacts and their stylistic details to trace external influences.

Certain parallels in terracotta figures of the Nok and other civilizations suggest cultural exchanges facilitated by trade. For instance, similar artistic expressions are found between the Nok and the later Yoruba culture to the southwest.

Moreover, the Nok figurine's details such as conical hats and lidded eyes are eerily similar to those found in sculptures from the ancient civilization of the Middle Niger. This points to external stylistic influences, possibly through trade interactions.

# 8.5. The Downfall and the Scattered Ashes

The downfall of the Nok civilization remains shrouded in mystery. Perhaps it was an environmental catastrophe, social unrest, or economic collapse. Yet another theory speculates that the depletion of wood due to the extensive smelting activities and terra-cotta figurine production could have led the civilization to its end.

Even in their downfall, there remain subtle traces of the Nok's trading prowess. As the Nok culture vanished around 200 AD, its stylistic influences lingered and seeped into neighboring terrains. This is seen in the artistic practices of subsequent civilizations, such as the Yoruba and Igbo tribes, and even as far as Cameroon.

Thus, the ashes of the Nok civilization were scattered far beyond the original confines of the Jos Plateau, testifying to a long and expansive trading network.

We may never fully grasp the intricacies of the Nok civilization or the extent of their trade networks. Yet, through the terra-cotta figurines and the echoes of their influence resonating in later cultures, we can perceive the ripples they sent through time, underscoring their pivotal role in the region's history. These shadows of the past, though fragmented, serve as a testament to a civilization that was, and reminds us of cultures that demand to be remembered.

# Chapter 9. Echoes from Prehistoric Mound Builders: North America's Anonymous Architects

In the fertile valleys of North America, stretching from the Appalachians to the Rockies, centuries before the arrival of Christopher Columbus, a complex and enigmatic civilization flourished, largely undetected and unrecorded in the annals of history. Ascribing a single name or tribal affiliation to these ancient architects is fraught with complications due to the geographic expanse and temporal span of their framework. For our purposes, we'll refer to these civilizations as the 'Mound Builders'— for the vast and diverse landscape punctuated with earthen mounds that they left behind is their most astounding legacy.

## 9.1. The Majestic Mounds: Gigantic Artistic Footprints

Their most potent and telling legacies, earthen mounds, straddle across North America, bearing silent testament to the architectural prowess of these prehistoric people. Rising from the earth in an assortment of shapes – from conical, cylindrical, to animal shapes these monumental earthen bulwarks hold a wealth of insights into their intriguing world.

The shapes and purposes of these mounds were as varied as their builders. Some mounds, like those at Poverty Point (c. 1500 BC), which represents some of the oldest mounds, are evocative of colossal earthworks laid out in complicated geometric models that extend for several miles. More recent mounds like those at Cahokia

(c. AD 1050) were stepped pyramids, often with flat summits which were platforms for significant structures.

Perhaps most intriguing and popular among these are the effigy mounds depicting birds, bears, and serpents. The 1,348-foot Serpent Mound in Ohio is perhaps the most famous of these effigies, its sinuous form suggesting the meanders of a river or the movements of a snake. Piled stone monuments, most notably the Great Stone Door in Tennessee, offer further variations of these earthworks.

Recent archaeological excavations have decoded that these sacred mounds probably functioned as diverse social, ceremonial, and burial sites. Their high-style pottery, exquisite textiles, dazzling copper weavings, and intricate shell carvings reveal much about their spiritual belief system.

# 9.2. Ciphers from the Soil: Unearthing the Mound Builders' Life

Archaeological excavations at these mound sites have yielded valuable clues to the life and times of these prehistoric people. Digs have unearthed tools, pottery, artefacts, seeds, carbonized wood and skeletal remains which give us a glimpse into their lifestyle, techniques, skills and diet.

Their technological innovations are evident in their artefacts and structures. Skilled artisans, they were adept at clay, stone, wood and bone. Copper mined from the Great Lakes region was hammered into splendid weaponry, tools, decorative ornaments and effigy figures. Beautiful ceramics – often decorated with complex designs – served practical purposes and ceremonial functions.

Food remains reveal a dynamic hunter-gatherer methodology with a relatively advanced progression towards agriculture. Analysis of plant remains suggests a shift from native plants towards the cultivation of squash, sunflower, goosefoot, and other crops. A substantial deposit of snail shells indicates a diet that incorporated diverse, local resources.

Not just a reflection of their civilization, these everyday remnants are timestamps telling the story of a sophisticated society very adept at modifying and making the best use of its environment.

## 9.3. Narratives Encoded in Art and Symbols

Equally intriguing is the symbolic and artistic tradition of the Mound Builders. Their ceramic, stone, and metal works reveal a rich symbolic language that narrates complex cosmologies, social hierarchies, and spiritual beliefs.

Similarities in motifs across vast geographies and generations hint at shared cultural threads or exchange networks. The infamous 'Birdman' motif represented in chert flint clay figurines found in the Great Mound at Cahokia depicts a man with a bird head, suggesting a key figure or deity in their mythology.

Images of weeping eyes, hand-and-eye motifs and intricate swirls carved into artefacts and embellishing pottery may convey metaphoric representations of cosmological beliefs or tales, as do the frequent combinations of terrestrial and celestial symbols.

## 9.4. The Demise of Mound Builders: An Unsolved Mystery

Despite their incredible architectural achievements and intricate artistry, the Mound Building cultures began to decline around 1400 AD. Numerous theories surround this mysterious collapse. A plausible theory posits drastic climate changes that disrupted agricultural practices, causing socio-economic unrest. Epidemic diseases due to changes in population density and diet is another possible factor.

Many mound sites were reoccupied by different Late Prehistoric cultures, who carried forward some aspects of the mound building traditions. Yet, the original Mound Builders' identities remain as obscure as their rapid decline. Their mounds, nevertheless, continue to stand, embodying a resilient past, asserting their presence in the silent chapters of human history.

As we still grapple to analyze the whispers of clay and shards of bone, the Mound Builders continue to tantalize archaeologists, historians, and enthusiasts alike. They compel us to ponder on the impermanence of civilization's structures and the permanence of its aspirations. This reality about the human race sparks a level of empathy and connection, creating an intimate narrative that is both universal and timeless. The echoes of these anonymous architects shall continue to reverberate across the hallways of history as long as these mounds touch the sky. They are an enduring testament to a people who, without the advantage of alphabets, etched their story on the bosom of the earth in an indelible handwriting of hills and mounds.

# Chapter 10. The Elamites: Unpuzzle The Language of The Past

The Elamites, one of the most mysterious civilizations of the ancient world, emerged around 3000 BC, in the region that is present-day Iran. Sprinkled across time and geographical extent, the imprints and evidence of their existence present an enigma, inviting researchers and scholars to dig deeper into the well-kept secrets of these ancient people through the lens of language.

## 10.1. Unearthing the Elamite Civilization

The Elamite civilization was situated in the southwestern region of ancient Iran, known as Khuzestan in modern day. Despite the adjoining Mesopotamian civilizations echoing their grandiosity through extensive documentation, the Elamite civilization remains an enigma primarily due to the complexities of their linguistic system. Their recorded history, spread over 2000 years, is divided into three principal periods: Old Elamite (c. 2600—1500 BC), Middle Elamite (c. 1500—1100 BC), and Neo-Elamite (c. 1100—539 BC). Though evidence exists of more than 100,000 inscriptions in the Elamite language, a plethora of questions surround the decipherment of this lost language.

## 10.2. Deciphering the Elamite Language

The Elamite language, among the oldest written languages, is a linguistic isolate, no certain relatives in any other recorded languages—much like the puzzling Basque language of Spain and France. This unique language was primarily written in the cuneiform script, which was adopted from neighboring Mesopotamian civilizations. The first to decode the Elamite cuneiform was Norwegian scholar, Jens Halvorson, in the late 19th century who discovered that Elamite cuneiform consisted of nearly 130 signs—roughly half of the signs used in Akkadian cuneiform. Even with this achievement, understanding of the script is far from complete due to the ambiguity and complexity of the signs.

The Elamite language comprises of three main dialects or versions - Old, Middle and Neo-Elamite, corresponding with the three principal periods of their civilizational history. Old Elamite texts are somewhat scarce, but the remaining documents represent a variety of genres. Whereas Middle and Neo-Elamite, despite several known inscriptions, remain ill-understood primarily due to grammatical complexities.

# 10.3. The Complex Linguistic Structure

The Elamite language had a Subject-Object-Verb (SOV) order, which was different from the Verb-Subject-Object (VSO) order used in Akkadian languages. Elamite lacks any known cognate language, inducing complications in unraveling their grammar system. Studies show peculiar characteristics about the Elamite language that set it apart. For example, it did not distinguish between gender, number, and had no tenses, but depicted cases particularly through suffixes. Moreover, it demonstrated use of extensive pronominal and verbal affixes, much like the agglutinative languages. Paradoxically, Elamite also exhibited signs of being an inflected language, further augmenting the complexity for linguists.

# 10.4. Elamite Inscriptions - The Key to the Past

Elamite inscriptions are mainly found on stone and metal. Major sources of Elamite texts include the collections of tablets found in Susa, Persepolis, and other sites in Iran. Prominent among them are the Persepolis Fortification and Treasury tablets, which have offered invaluable insights into the social, economic, and administrative aspects of the Persian Empire.

The bilingual and trilingual inscriptions have been vital for deciphering and translating Elamite language. For instance, the trilingual inscription of Behistun, carved on a cliff in western Iran, was instrumental in finally cracking the Elamite script. Inscribed in Old Persian, Babylonian, and Elamite, it presented nearly identical accounts, paving the way for comparative translation efforts.

# 10.5. The Unsolved Mysteries of Elamite Language

Despite our advancements in understanding this ancient language, many inconsistencies and unknowns still exist in the Elamite language. An appreciation of the finer nuances of the language, the finer points of vocabulary and grammar, remains an uphill task. Further complicating matters is the absence of a bilingual lexicon and irregular application of phonetic values, leaving much conjecture about pronunciation and interpretation.

Understanding Elamite, a civilizational tongue that flourished thousands of years ago, is no less than decoding history itself. The legacy of this forgotten yet remarkable civilization continues to weave enigmas resolved patiently by scholars. It's indeed a lesson of human endurance to reach through time, us trying to listen and understand the whispers of our past, the thoughts that once populated minds as vivid and eager as ours. Every word deciphered, every sentence understood, is a tribute to that burning human instinct—to explore, to understand, to be remembered.

In conclusion, while the Elamites civilization might be lost to the sands of time, the echo of their language continues to resonate in the pages of human history. To unravel and comprehend the Elamite language is to voyage down the memory lane of human civilization, decoding the intriguing mysteries held within those ancient ciphers—the symbols embodying a quintessential part of our shared legacy. The story of the Elamites is a testament to our ever-enduring strive for understanding the whispers of the forgotten.

# Chapter 11. From Obscurity to Light: The Future of Uncovering the Past

From the secrecy of forgotten vaults to the limelight of academic discovery, the passion to unlock the secrets of past civilizations has been an enduring intrigue that has spurred human curiosity through the ages. As we venture into the promising future of archaeological endeavours, every artefact unearthed stands not just as a relic of the past, but as a beckoning voyage through our shared human story.

## 11.1. Innovation in Archaeology

Accelerating scientific and technological advancements have been revolutionizing the field of archaeology. Gone are the days of relying solely on excavation and intuition. Today, we stride forward with remote sensing technologies, aerial surveys, ground penetrating radar, satellite imaging, and Lidar (Light Detection and Ranging) to uncover the hidden treasures of the past.

Lidar, for instance, has been particularly transformative in archaeological exploration. Using lasers from aircrafts or drones, Lidar measures the distance to the ground, creating detailed topographic maps that can reveal previously unseen or inaccessible structures. This technology helped uncover the vast suspended network of cities in the ancient Maya civilization, championing a new era of discovery.

3D scanning and printing hold immense potential for archaeology too. They allow us to digitally capture, reproduce and study fragile artefacts in ways that were previously unimaginable. Every groove, every notch, and every mark on an artefact can now be examined in detail without risking damage to the original piece.

## 11.2. Piecing Together the Puzzle

But the language of the past is incomplete without the translation of scripts. Decrypting ancient texts is akin to finding a Rosetta Stone for each civilization. With machine learning algorithms, we're now tackling this task with unmatched precision. These algorithms can recognize and decipher patterns in ancient scripts, facilitating the understanding of extinct languages and, in turn, lost cultures.

An area where AI comes particularly in handy is in predicting the progression of artefacts in time. Dating ancient relics is essential in understanding the chronology and context of historical events, and with the aid of machine learning algorithms, we are capable of creating more accurate timelines.

## 11.3. Enhancing Public Engagement Through Virtual Reality

Increasingly, we've also begun to employ virtual and augmented reality platforms in archaeology. Through these cutting-edge technologies, we can now recreate ancient cities, rituals, and daily life scenarios for a wider audience, providing the opportunity to travel through time and space, and "experience" history as it unfolds.

## 11.4. Eradicating Looting and Illicit Trafficking

Despite our technological strides, challenges persist. Looting remains a grave issue that can result in significant loss of historical information. Illicit trafficking of artefacts robs not only the countries of origin but humanity as a whole of our shared cultural heritage. However, digital technology, including databases, satellite imaging, and modern tracking tools, are constantly being developed to help authorities respond to and curtail these illegal activities.

# 11.5. Popularity of Underwater Archaeology

Looking ahead, underwater archaeology is poised to be one of the most exciting frontiers of exploration. The ocean floors hold untold riches of yesteryears, waiting to be discovered. While challenging, the advances in sonar mapping, remotely operated underwater vehicles (ROVs), and deep-sea diving technology, offer the potential to uncover a plethora of sunken cities, shipwrecks, and submerged settlements.

# 11.6. Inclusivity in Archaeology

A future of archaeological discovery also calls for greater inclusivity and diversity. A range of perspectives from a culturally diverse team can offer more nuanced and comprehensive interpretations of the relics of the past. Moreover, involving the local communities in archaeological projects fosters a sense of ownership of their heritage and aids in its preservation.

As the chronicles of time continue to unfurl, the coming chapters of discovery shall undoubtedly be filled with renewed passion for uncovering the past. We now stand equipped with smarter tools, innovative methodologies, and bright minds. The exploration of ancient civilizations, once shrouded in mystery, is being illuminated by the torch of modern science. The whispers of the forgotten resonate in the relics strewn across the facades of time, waiting eagerly to be heard and understood.

Our journey from obscurity to the illumination of the past promises to be as thrilling as it is enlightening. As Robert Louis Stevenson rightly said, "We are all travellers in the desert of the world, and the best we can find on our journey is an honest friend." Let us be those honest friends, those devoted travellers, earnestly seeking, listening, and unearthing stories of a shared history that has been waiting in the shadows, a testament to our collective past and a beacon for our shared future.

www.ingramcontent.com/pod-product-compliance
Lightning Source LLC
La Vergne TN
LVHW051633050326
832903LV00033B/4743